A Poet's Dream

A Poet's Dream

Earlisteen "Dink" Simpson

A collection of christian poetry

XULON PRESS

Xulon Press
2301 Lucien Way #415
Maitland, FL 32751
407.339.4217
www.xulonpress.com

© 2019 by Earilsteen Dink Simpson

All rights reserved solely by the author. The author guarantees all contents are original and do not infringe upon the legal rights of any other person or work. No part of this book may be reproduced in any form without the permission of the author. The views expressed in this book are not necessarily those of the publisher.

Printed in the United States of America.

ISBN-13: 978-1-54565-865-9

Dedication

"These poems in this book have inspired me thru the years to be creative and become enriched for keeps." They have also been rewarding and fun too. The poem "The Servant brings Salvation" at the beginning describes the Geneses of Art by my life forces. I dedicate this Book to my husband Steve, son Stephen, also my sister Wanda who has supported me and who believed in me and my poetry ages ago. Without their love and support these passages and poetry possibly would not have been written. The Patterson Baptist Sunday School Class Poetry "was written with love for members of our "Faith" class of which I am a part of."

From all this: "I have become a "Partaker of His Devine Nature." 2 Peter 1:4

Acknowledgements

"How thankful I am to Christ Jesus our Lord
For considering me trustworthy and
Appointing me to serve Him-"
I wish most particularly to thank, Sandra Whitaker,
A dear friend, who took overall the
Publication details and helped make this
Journey a reality.
A hearty thank you to my sister, Wanda,
Who believed in my poetry ages ago.
And in closing, Thank you, "Sandy," for your
Design and layout of making this journey
Very much fulfilled.

THE SERVANT BRINGS SALVATION

"For He has clothed me with the garments
of Salvation and wrapped me in a robe of
Righteousness… as a bride adorns herself
with her jewels"

"Lord," I voiced, "I want to be Your servant
not the poet; so unto You I bestow
my pad, my jewels – even my vest."

Now satisfied and delighted, she returned with a smile
and sung to herself, "Awake, awake; put on strength,
put on beautiful clothes. For the original and pure
will no longer enter His courts with praise."

Still not a minute has passed by since the end
of time that anyone has composed a new creation
so smoothly – also nobody grand will ever enter into it,
and no one who does what is disgraceful or unfit;
till now only those written in the Lamb's Book of Life.

Just give her a pen – a soul ready to charge it off
and she'll tender ev'ryone with an imagination –
a melody well-favored that a fire would-be revived
where their naturally flesh and blood;
while her spirit will be well-informed at all-time.

So, she jumped across her pad and waved her arms
in the air; Its absent not to be open,
"I reflectedth our savors were sound"
But it's absolutely worthy of this creation
to understand the rest of the drama
that the cross isn't about withdrawals and
Christ's love can't be beat;
oh yes, Thank you, Lord, for Your love, kindness
and providing the key to the solution!

How wonderful I have Salvation reenkindled –
now I will gracefully sing of His love, forevermore.
In Jesus' precious name, Amen.

A Song of Praise unto the Son

Behold, All ye believers, Hallelujah! Praise the name of the Lord; Give praise, you servants of the Lord

Therefore, dear friends, from right this minute on:
"And so, let's strengthen ourselves in jealous care,
As with thy sight to fulfill an obligation;
Also with Thy servants, Lord, render a sizable gift,
Throughout gratitude into each one's hearts;
Absolutely, servants, from the rising of the sun
 onto it's setting, let the name of the Lord be praised;
Yes, give praise to the all-merciful God, O servants
of the Lord; praise the name of the Lord!
O thank you, Lord, for Your goodness, tenderness
And my new life in Christ!"

How vividly I have Salvation undergone –
now I will gracefully sing of His love, forevermore
in Jesus' divine name, we pray, amen

Ascended Like No Other

Never alone; yet
Even height through His presence. Now
Validating all; so, let nothing
Even love keep us apart. Still I shall
Rise and go with peace of mind.
                Dink Simpson

A Tender Symphony unto out Father

Behold, All ye believers, "He will yet fill your mouth with laughter and your lips with shouts of joy."

Therefore, dear friends, from right this hour on:
still angels sing on! Our faithful views beginning,
sing ev'ryone tender savors of the symphony above;
Till down's rapture evenly defines a night of rejoicing.
While life's clear-cut blinds sets invisible love;
Angels of Jesus, angels of light, singing to welcome
The voyagers of the night;
Angels of Jesus, angels of light, singing to welcome
The voyagers of the night;
absolutely admirers, let's hold onto the hope that
we hath, for our cup with His many blessings o'erflows
oh yes, Thank You, Lord, for Your love, forgiveness
And my new life in Christ!

How sophisticated I have Salvation reenlivened -
Now I will gracefully sing of His love, forevermore
In Jesus' divine name, we pray, Amen.

Spiritual Renewal

High Spirits

Aeropause

Pleasure

Playfulness

Yelling

Newness

Enlightenment

Winning

Year

Existence

Accomplishment

Rejoicing

A Song of Praise unto our Savior

Into His hands we entrust our souls;
You have redeemed us, Lord, God of light,
Redirect us in Spirit and truth
As You are the God who saves everyone
Sill we rest beside You the full day
Your eyes are on the divine and Your ears are open to our voices in care
Naturally, we are not ashamed of the gospel;
Because we believe, and we are certain
That nothing can ever change our Conduct
For the softhearted;
Therefore, let's take up the gospel and
Behold the return of His hands.
How sensational I have Salvation undergone –
Now I will joyfully sing with our Savior.

A Tender Melody unto the Son

Behold, All ye believers, "For I know the plans I have for you, this is the Lord's declaration – plans for your welfare, not for disaster, to give you a future and a hope."

Hereafter, dear friends, from right now on:
Still encourage e'eryone to watch and pray, Lord,
As throughout Thy Spirit remaining;
Reassured also, if our melody goes alongside,
O may it always fulfill our Master's will;
Absolutely, devotees, if God so loved the world
Within this way, Surely, we must uphold His good
Works and His intentions for the other Souls as well;
Yes, Thank You, Lord, for Your love, friendship
And my new life in Christ!

How sensational I have Salvation restored –
Now I will gracefully Sing of His love, forevermore.
In Jesus' divine name, we pray, Amen.

Christ is Born

Hear the bells ringing
They're singing that Jesus Christ is born
Hear the bells ringing
They're singing Christ the savior is born

The angels on top of the mountain
Sang, "It came upon the midnight clear!
Still singing, go tell of His excellent greatness
That Jesus Christ is born."

With peace on earth, good will to men!
Praise Him! Praise Him! Ever in joyful song!
How still we see the light.
Rapidly now, that Jesus Christ is born.

"Praying for Ourselves"

I want to thank You and praise You, Lord,
For giving us today our daily bread.
I am absolutely inspired upon You
To enrich me to-date to live the life
You want me to live and to tender the Songs
You've called me to perform.
I choose to dwell in You hour by hour:
Still I plead You to recreate reformation
The utmost rhythm written on my heart,
Your truth, God, the perfect motivations
And desired before all we rejoiced.
Your peace and harmony
The rapture roundabout all I wish to achieve.
I plead You to favor ev'ryone within good grace
O'erall kind of sin.
I plead You to recite Your wonderous works
In our souls and in our voices;
Even so, I want to thank You, Lord,
For Your love and forgiveness!
In Jesus' divine name, we pray, Amen.
PS. 40:3a (KJV) And He hath put a new song in my mouth, even praise unto our God.

"A Tender Verse unto God"

O praise the tide of grace
That unfolded at every shore
Throughout visions of a universe resting
No deeper love rendered by sound:
O praise the tide of grace
Yet much more than these, O praise its lightness,
Praise Christ the purified:
Praise Christ! praise Christ! praise Christ!
Praise Christ! Whose cross have left all awake
Still having foreseen this in the beginning,
As His only Son within whom He made them
Most welcome into the tides of the sea.
How wonderful I have Salvation reenkindled –
Now I will gratefully Sing of His love, forever
In Jesus' divine name, Amen

"Gracious Hospitality"

To live gratified without great fines;
To create beauty instead of imagination,
And grace instead of freedom,
To be worthy, not hospitable.
And rich, not wealthy;
To learn tenderly, reflect absolutely, voice lovingly,
To listen to birds and stars,
To sages and angels, with all one's heart;
To bear upon all joyfully, perform al willingly,
Foresee the times, divine always;
In a verse, to welcome the Spiritual, unsound
And unique, redirect in gracious hospitality;
Even so, that is to be our Symphony from now on,
As the Lord Jesus Christ has come
With ten thousand of His holy ones!

                    Hebrews 13:2
Be not forgetful to entertain strangers; for thereby some have entertained angels unawares.

A Christmas Chant

Behold, the glory of the Lord
Shone round about them;
Then everyone rapturously voiced,
And started chanting:
Return, o wonderous perfect light, return!
Bring forth this day, our Savior Jesus Christ,
Whom shall be to all people of the nations;
O shephards, tremble not with fear,
Still many naturally overheard the angels greeting!
This newborn, now tender by birth,
Our hope and merrymaking shall remain,
The power of Satan breaking,
Bringing about our rest eternal drawing.
How sensational I have salvation rendered –
Now I will gracefully sing of His love, forever more.
In Jesus' divine name, we pray, amen.

Have a Merry Christmas!
2017

A New Song to Him

'Twas joy I chased, Found harmony and peace;
Then again we see, Bestow what is friendship.
Now all out note is: May the grace of the
Lord Jesus Christ, the love of God, and the
fellowship of the Holy Spirit be
with all of us. Forever and forever more.

Earlisteen "Dink" Simpson

"The True Light of the World"

Behold, All believers, "That light shines in the
Darkness, yet the darkness did not grasp it."

Therefore, dear friends, from right now on:
Still when trials are dark on ev'ry hand and
We can't seem to uphold all the passages
That God led ev'ryone alongside;
As He guides them with His eye and
We're caught composing it altogether,
Naturally, we'll understand it better by and by,
When the morning tenders the start of the day
Throughout the true light of the world;
Absolutely, devotees, God is light an there is
No darkness in Him at all; Also we'll tell the story
How we o'ercame hour after hour and follow
'Til we perform;
Oh yes, thank You, Lord, for Your love, forgiveness
An my new life in Christ. Yours is the Spirit!
How wonderful I have Salvation enlightened –
Now I will gracefully sing of His love, forevermore.
In Jesus' precious name, Amen.

"A Hymn of Gratitude"

Grace followers, behold! God publicly endorsed
Jesus by doing wonderful miracles, wonders
And signs in Him as e'eryone understands.
Yet He will return!
We know You are always with us, Lord,
We will not be shaken, for You are beside us
No wonder our cups are o'erflowing with joy,
And our voices singing Your praises!
Still our Spirits rest within pastures of
Tender grass, for You would not allow our souls
To quaver or allow Your chosen ones to tremble
Among the living, You have led us in paths
of righteousness and You have rendered them
wonderful joy thro' Him;
Absolutely, let it be known that we, followers,
Are carrying our cross up-to-date and
Following Him;
Oh yes, Thank You, Lord, for your love, friendship
And my new life in Christ!
How inspiring I have Salvation reenchanted –
Now I will gratefully sing of Thy love, forevermore
In Jesus' divine name, Amen.

To the Great One in Three

To the great one in Three, The highest praises be
O Lord, again we find, Given to adoration;
Now all our Song is: Glory be to Jesus!
Glory be to Jesus! Glory be to Jesus!
God in three Persons, blessed Trinity!
Glory be to Jesus. Forever and at the last tone.

Patriotic Song

Thy finest hour by far
Upon Him be pleased to reflect;
Long may He author:
May He protect us by Thy might,
And always render us light
To sing within heart and voice,
Great God, our King!

"Brotherly Love"

Compassion should be the passage an imagination
Of our well-being;
Compassion, ever tenders or unites,
Yet willfully, loving and natural;
The performing of work, never absolutely
That the work wilt be to all who are
Within our path;
As yet into my heart: Still in upholding
It shalt become agreeable to foreseeing
Brotherly love and embracing the Father,
Son, and Holy Spirit!

Psalm 133:1

Behold, how good and how pleasing it is for brethren to dwell together in unity!

"The Lord our Protector"

Behold, All believers, "Shall I lift up mine eyes
To the hills? Whence should help come?"

Therefore, dear friend, from right minute:
Still we'll raise our eyes unto Him the One
Enthroned within heav'n;
For Thy rock is upon the holy mountains,
For You, Lord, our God, protects ev'ryone
Throughout all harm, While You also safeguard our lives;
Absolutely, Christians, from ev'ry mountain side,
Let's tender the glory of our return,
As we live for Him ev'ryday;
Oh yes, Thank You, Lord, for Your Love, forgiveness
And my new Life in Christ!

How sensational I have Salvation encouraged –
Now I will gracefully sing of His love, forevermore,
In Jesus' divine name, we pray, amen.

With An Artistic Design

O most beautiful of women!
Let's go out into green pastures.
And foresee all our good works.
Still let a search be directed for
The soft one.
How wonderful is our Savior's love –
Now I will return singing for us.

"The Giving of Gifts"

Behold, All believers, "Based on the gift they have
Received, everyone should use it to serve others,
As good managers of the varied grace of God."

Therefore, dear friends, from right now on:
Still we'll tell the world of His saving grace,
Making well-known within ev'ry hour;
Encouraging the prosperous ones to praise Him
From Whom all blessing flow, O Savior divine;
So, let's ring it out, ring it out! ring it out!
As He naturally delights for the Spirit
He formed to live through me;
Absolutely, devotees, let's chant the message
Tenderly, while He's making them happy and free;
Oh yes, Thank You, Lord, for Your love, kindness
And Your message of divination. Yours is the Spirit!

How vivid I have Salvation reenlivened -
Now I will gratefully Sing of His love, forevermore.
In Jesus' glorious name, Amen.

"The Love of Jesus"

Return, let us retell God's beautiful love
It flows over like waves from out of the blue
We can't escape it, try as we shall
Yet it will pull at our feet, eternal to rest
His love is for everyone of us
To Sing it, He died upon the Cross
His love will hold every joy we feel
We foretold the future, we foretold the facts
His love is like the brightest moon
O direct us far or near
Tell God that you trust Him now
Come into His arms O Sinner, come home.

A Song of Praise Unto God

First abov**E** all, let us praise

The risen king! "**A**lleluia" Sing!

For He hath ri**S**en! He overcame

dea**T**h! He's risen!

Now within th**E** blink of an eye,

Let's g**R**acefully sing of His love!

Have a Happy Easter

"Behold the Lamb"

You, the Lamb
Oh Soft one,
My heart doth Sing
He shall our Song unroll.
He has foreseen us through the night,
Through the day
And even as He looks over us
Or ever when there is no light
He is our friend
Unto the very end
He is the one who created us
He knew that we
Were not faithful
How happy I have salvation undergone –
Now I will return Singing with Him.

"The Lord Is our Righteousness"

Behold, All ye believers, "Call to me and I will answer you and tell you great and incomprehensible things you do not know."

Therefore, dear friends, from this day forward:
While He return throughout trumpet sound,
O, let us now in Him be seen,
Clothed within righteousness and His faith alone,
Of course trembling to bear all before the throne!
And so, believers, this is His name:
"The Lord Is our Righteousness"
Absolutely, there is hope for e'eryone up-do-date,
The kind of trust we need to redeem our souls;
Oh yes, let's Hear Him today, hear Him today!

How dramatic I have Salvation enlightened –
Now I will gracefully Sing of His love, forevermore
In Jesus' divine name, we pray, Amen.

A Pause for Silence

MeMorial Day recalled:

For HE clearly knows what

We are Made of,

Still recOgnizing too that

We aRe made of dust;

For He also recognIzed that they were

Only flesh, An air that blows fully overall,

But doesn't render saLute within good faith.

2017

A Tender Chant unto our King

Behold, All ye believers, "And now, all glory to God, who is able to keep you from stumbling, and who will welcome you into His glorious presence innocent of sin and with great joy."

Hereafter, Christians, from this minute on:
O trust our loving Savior and Sail alongside
With us in that heavenly way;
Then quickly we'll be Singing a tender chant
At home within the Kingdom light of day;
O meet us there, yes, meet us there,
Where life is so grand and pure; so grand and pure
Naturally, we long for e'eryone to be welcome too!
O promise to meet me there;
Absolutely, devotees, now to the only God,
Our loving savior, be glory, majesty, power, and authority always!

How wonderful I have Salvation of His love, forevermore
In Jesus' divine name, we pray, amen.

How Great Our Joy

Softened by the sheep we foretold again
Good tidings overflowing and angel bright
How great our joy! Great our joy!
Joy, joy, joy! Joy, joy, joy!
O God, in heaven most high!
O God, in heaven most high!
Surely, that goodness our hearts
Fulfilled through Your love for all of us.

"The Lord Raised Me"

Behold, Christians, "Having been set free from sin you became enslaved to righteousness."

Therefore, All believers, from here on after:
I have a friend who is all the world to me
His love is ever so absolute
I love to tell her how He raised me.
And what His love wilt do for e'eryone;
While on the peaceful shore to day,
Praises joy I sung, sinful days have past beyond
Unto the Lord, I hold; Within it His marvelous
Light I breathe, pure, sweet and free;
Naturally throughout the world I rejoice!
The Lord raised me! The Lord raised me!
The Lord raised me! The Lord raised me!
O whispered free indeed and made me whole!
Even so, If God loved us by this ne way,
Surely, we also must love one another!

How sensational I have Salvation reenraptured –
Now I will gracefullt Sing of His love, forevermore.
In Jesus' precious name, Amen.

A Tender Verse unto God

Behold, All ye believers, "Remember your leaders who
have spoken God's word to you. As you carefully observe
the outcome of your life, imitate your faith."

Therefore, dear friends, from here on after:
Still, beloved, when you know our blest Savior,
Naturally all our pleasures will turn alongside,
Just like within the fog before the sunset,
At the tendering of the day!
Howe'er when you know Him! When you know Him!
You will love our Savior as well;
When you know Him, O How you'll love Him;
When you know how He loves and cares for e'eryone
Absolutely, Let's not imitate what is evil,
But what is good;
Oh yes, let's share our Master's joy throughout all we sing!
How vividly I have salvation reenforced –
Now I will gracefully Sing of His love, forevermore.
In Jesus' divine name, we pray, amen.

"Rejoice In Reality"

Behold, All ye believers, "For I am the Lord Your God who stirs up the sea so that its waves roar – His name is the Lord of the armies"

Therefore, dear friends, from right now on:
Still theirs a very high price to uphold we
Tenderly own, a God to praise, a infinite
Soul to keep and fit for the seas;
Absolutely, admirers, more than all jewels thy
Spirit is real! God, the creator, has given it originality
And so, believers, what would you give? What would you
give in exchange for your soul? What would you give?
Oh, if this hour, God, need be nearby;
What would you give in exchange for your soul?
Even now, Lord, I just want to thank You for
Your love and for weighing in the balances with me!

How sensational I have Salvation regenerated -
Now I will gracefully Sing of His love, forevermore.
In Jesus' divine name, we pray, Amen.

A Song of God's Love

Joyfully, joyfully the angels sing,
"Try a little tenderness!" For still we
  Overhear them singing and through the night
  Their echoes softly ringing;
Till now singing a little verse.
Because today overflows with praise of God's love.

"Love Song"

Behold, all ye believers, "As for God, His way is perfect.
The word of the Lord is refined: He is a anchor to all who trust in Him"

Therefore, dear friends, from right now on:
Even so, "Let not your hearts become concerned,"
For this tenderhearted song we already heard;
But now we can only rest upon his friendship,
As we softened our divination and originality;
Atho' into the passage He directeth, Still throughout
That one step we understand full well:
As He will cover them with His feathers,
And within Thy wings wilt He entrust;
O His eye is on the dove and we know
He cares for them;
Absolutely, devotes, we sing cause we're happy,
We sing cause we're free, for His eye is on
The dove and we know He guards overall of us;
Oh yes, Thank You, Lord, for Your love, forgiveness
And my new life in Christ!
How sophisticated I have Salvation reenkindled –
Now I will gracefully Sing of His love, forevermore.
In Jesus' divine name, Amen.

A Tender Verse unto God

Behold, All believers, oh, The praises of e'erybody
who foresees shelter in Christ Jesus!
Still You, O Lord, is a shield around them,
And the One who lifts up their souls
High overall the others:
You have heard them with their own voices
From Your holy mountain!
Hereby rendering them unique blessings,
And taking along their trust in You;
Absolutely, allowing the smile of Your face, Lord,
To shine on them as well;
Cause You have tendered them greater rapture
Than the rest who had even at grace time;
Oh yes, Thank You, Lord, for Your love, kindness
And my new life in Christ!

How wonderful I have Salvation reenraptured –
Now I will gratefully Sing of His love, forevermore
In Jesus' divine name, Amen.

A Tender Verse Unto the Son

Belo**V**ed, let us continue

To love one **A**nother

For **L**ove is within God

And **E**veryone who loves

Has been bor**N**e of Him and knows Him

Na**T**urally we have rendered

Th**I**s verse gracefully from

The beginn**N**ing: that we must

Love on**E** another.

2018

All in All

Since we are all one in Christ we must also put on love;
For love is what binds us all together in perfect Harmony.
                                          Dink Simpson

"Rhapsody"

Behold, All Christians, "Your real life is hidden with Christ in God and when Christ is Revealed to the whole world, you will share In all His glory."

Therefore, dear friends, from here on after:
Still we're a joint heir always, with our Savior,
unto the Kingdom yonder;
Naturally we' go alongside to enjoin the happy
Angel band, where raptures ne'er tender;
Absolutely, devotees, 'til we meet on this side,
we have a mansion waiting that's much greater,
where we can share His goods nearby;
oh yes, let's keep Standing for the rest – and
Let's Keep Sailing! For we know that God is
At work within our melodious Songs!

How Spectacular I have Salvation borne –
Now I will gracefully Sing of His love, forevermore
In Jesus' divine name, we pray, Amen.

"Serenata"

The sea a very deep blue,
The earth of greenish gold tones,
The open air of ever so much tenderness,
The sun throughout Single-minded focus,
The fruit trees within bloom,
The days soaring and nights returning;
Did you know – how the days prolonged,
or how the nights gracefully o'erflowed as well,
Still we might wonder it's somewhat amazing,
Absolutely, It all embraces God's Divination;
Oh yes, Thank You, Lord, for Your love, forgiveness
And my new life in Christ!

How dramatizing I have Salvation reenlightened
Now I will gratefully Sing of His love, forevermore
In Jesus' divine name, we pray, Amen.

Connected in Christ

Because of our love and faith in Christ; We also rejoice in knowing every good thing through the Holy Spirit.

There is that goodness and Love
Burn within me, fire of God
Burn till I exist no more
Burn within me, fire of God
Burn till Your ears can overhear
our own trembling voice. Strongly and
surely formed through Your love for us.

"A Spiritual Song"

Behold, Lord, Hear our prayers and listen to our pleads
Heartened us, O Lord, we pray, to shed Your light
Refined, to rich and poor, to high and low
Of ev'ry people and kind;
O may Your flaming zeal burn
Absolutely and pure;
Till Souls within darkness e v'rywhere
Fall down and worship You;
Still teach us, Lord, to render Your perfect will,
Cause You are our God;
Also, may Your gracious Spirit
Lead ev'ryone along the right paths!

How wonderful I have Salvation reenkindled –
Now I will gracefully Sing of His love, forevermore.
In Jesus' precious name, Amen.

Dink Simpson

"The Music of the Zodiacs"

It is well with my soul
While this singing voice
All around me understands
The music of the Zodiacs

It is well with my soul
We rest upon an extended view
Of rocks and billows
His fingers the touch already taking effect

It is well with my soul
He shines in all that has been created,
Throughout the whispers of the song,
He sings to everyone in a imaginative way

It is well with my soul
"O come all ye faithful"
Even tho' the light seems original
Always so grand and pure
Jesus is the Master Still

It is well with my soul
The making is not yet absolute,
Christ who rose lives on;
For now, It is well with my soul!

Eagle's Introduction

Hear the soaring that eagles bear –
Soft the eye and coast alongside
of wig sun's touching with love;
Repeated within sight
of a glorious light
As long as life endures.

Softened

Merry Christmas

T**H**is is real love.

Dea**R** friend, let us

Cont**I**nue to love one another

for love come**S** from God. He has given

us his spiri**T** as proof that we live

in hi**M** and he in us. For

the F**A**ther sent his son

to be the **S**avior of the world.

"Within Good Grace"

God understand our thoughts from afar,
our heart's direction
our deepest love
And our every turn.

God always observes everyone's travels.
If we take up the wings of the morning;
And dwell by the farthest oceans
Behold, Thou art nearby!
For we can never escape His Spirit.

So, keep this love softened inside your heart
Reflect overall today, tomorrow, and forever;
If something comes along
That makes you foretell once more,
Recall the love carved inside your heart.

Oh, yes! Thank You, Lord, for making me
So absolutely unique,
Still point out anything in me that
Offends You and lead me beside peaceful streams!

Showing God's Love

Most important of all, continue to show deep love for each other, for love covers a multitude of sins.

Dink Simpson

A Tender Serenade unto our Father

Behold, All ye believers, "I am certain that I will see The Lord's goodness in the land of the living"

Therefore, dear friends, from this minute on:
Yet, how tender it will be, when those bright lights
We see, welcoming loved one's who've gone on before;
we will faint at His feet at His feet as His praises resounds,
Blessed Savior we'll love and adore….
What a wonderful place, we'll see by His grace
Within our pads and passages, written with Silver!
In this bright home below we'll reflect upon
All unique things, while the hours roll….
Absolutely, our hearts and souls may tremble,
But God is the rock of our hearts, always;
Even so, Lord, I will wait, only, for You
Wait, Silently, for You!

How dramatic I have Salvation reenfreshed –
Now I will gracefully Sing of His love, forevermore
In Jesus' precious name, Amen.

A Tender Melody unto God

Behold, All believers, "Even when I go through the valley of the Shadow of death, I fear no danger"

Hereafter, dear friends, from right now on:
Still we'll join our Savior there, Savior there,
If Jesus Himself shall be our Leader, we Shall
Go thro' the valley in peace, we shall go through
The valley of the Shadow of death, we shall go
Thro' the valley in peace; If Jesus Himself
Shall be our Leader, we shall go thro' the valley
In peace;
Absolutely, devotees, For the Lord is our light
And our Salvation – So why Should we fear?
Yea, The Lord is for us, So we will not fear:
What can mere mortals do with e'eryone?

oh yes, Thank You, Lord for Your love, forgiveness
And my new life in Christ!

How vivid I have Salvation refreshed –
Now I will gracefully Sing of His love, forevermore.
In Jesus' divine name, we pray, Amen.

A Tender Rhapsody unto God

Behold, All ye believers, "Remind everyone to be yielding
to rulers and authorities, to obey, to always be ready-made
for every good luck."

Therefore, dear friends, from right now on:;
Still theirs a bright day coming, A bright day coming,
Theirs a bright day returning;
But its tenderness can clearly remain within all those
Who befriend the Lord, Are you ready? Are you read
For that judgement day?
Absolute, devotees, for God saved us, not by
The fine works that we had done, but according
To His mercy;
Oh yes, Thank You, Lord, for Your kindness, love
And my life through His Holy Spirit!

How sophisticated I have Salvation regenerated -
Now I will gracefully Sing of His love, forevermore
In Jesus' precious name, Amen.

O Praise the Lord

Return the joy of thy Salvation
And uphold us with thy Free Spirit
Still we trust in thy unfailing love
Forevermore.
Therefore our hearts shall rejoice in Him.
Now I will joyfully Sing unto the Lord
All the earth.
Dink Simpson

A Tender Chant unto our King

Behold, All ye believers, "The one who lives honestly,
Practices righteousness and acknowledges The truth in
his heart –"

Therefore, dear friends, from now on:
Still in faith we Sing joyous praises unto Him,
Also within upright hearts we recite tenderness
And harmony;
Praise unto God, Sea of love, praise from mourn
Till the setting of the Sun;
Praise at home, praise in worship,
Praise unto God ev'rywhere on earth;
Absolutely, let each one walk uprightly,
Work diligently and voice the truth
Within their hearts;
oh yes, Thank you, Lord, for pouring out
Your love and blessings upon me!

How distinctively I have Salvation undergone –
Now I will gracefully Sing of His love, forevermore.
In Jesus' divine name, we pray, amen.

A Tender Chant unto the Father

Therefore, dear friends, from right this hour:
Still our Father is rich in pads and passages,
He holdeth the wealth of the universe in His palms
of diamonds or rubies, of gold or silver,
His baskets are unique, He has riches unforeseen;
Absolutely, with Jesus our Savior still we'll Sing:
All glory to God, we're a believer of the King!
A believer of the King! a believer of a King!
With Jesus our Savior, we're a believer of the King;
O in any case, whate'er its holding you back
This hour, God will distinctively provide the cups
O'erflowing with His many blessings;
Oh yes, Thank You, Lord, for Your love, kindness
And my new life in Christ!

How vividly I have a Salvation borne –
Now I will gracefully Sing of His love, forevermore
In Jesus' divine name, we pray, Amen.

Faithfulness

Trust in the Lord and do
What is good;
Dwell in the land and sow
Faithfulness
                  Dink Simpson

A Sentimental Letter unto God

Behold, All believers, And when the tempter came
To Him, he said, "If thou be the Son of God
Command that these stones be made bread."

Therefore, dear friends, from right now on:
Still as we're celebrating His great work
Ev'ry passing hour, what but by Thy Amazing grace
Can tender the tempter's power?
Absolutely, who unlike thyself, our Guide and hold
Wilt be? Thro' billow and flame, o abide with me
Naturally Singing glorifies and perfect peace praises
In life, in death, O Lord, with me abide!
So, let's not imitate what is the blues,
But what is, surely, Complete likeness;
Oh yes, let's take up His cross daily,
And follow in His footsteps till we see Jesus!

How vivid I have Salvation reenkindled –
Now I will gratefully Sing of His love, forevermore
In Jesus' glorious name, amen.

Hope through God's Mercy

God is wonderfully good unto all
Who wait for Him, to the soul who
Searcheth Him.
Yes, its good to rest calmly
In righteousness from Christ our Lord.
Still, its joyfully good to oversee
The very soft upon the renewing
of His direction.
     Dink Simpson

"A Tender Melody unto the Shephard"

The Lord is my inspiration, I shall not race,
He allows me leisure and breath for healing,
He grants me with reflections of softness
That restores my Spirit;
He leads me in paths of righteousness
Throughout peace of mind,
And His direction is love;
Even tho' I have a good many things
To complete up-to-the minute,
I'll not mind for His presence is nearby;
His return, His all-impressions
will uphold me in taking rest,
He provides restoration and revival
Deep inside the well of my being,
While satisfying my soul within His essences
of fortitude,
my cup of raptures delight o'erflows;
Absolutely, harmony and grace
Shalt pursue me all the days of my life,
And I will dwell in His house, forevermore.
In Jesus' precious name, Amen!

A Love Song

Regeneration and renewal through the Spirit; Still
Echoing joyfully in our awakening Souls, and
Everyone again to return to Him. O Lord,
Will You not fill each heart with Thy love.
                              Dink Simpson

A Song of Worship unto the Father

Behold, All ye believers, "Before the Passover Festival,
Jesus knew His hour had come to depart from
This world to the Father. Having loved His own
Who were in the world, He loved them completely."

Therefore, dear friends, from right this minute on:
Still is their anyone that will uphold you.
Altho' raptures tender your souls?
O unlike sea billows rolling alongside as well;
Even if we need a friend to restore our souls,
Yes, there's one, only one, the blessed, blessed Jesus
He's the one;
Absolutely, devotees, Now glory be to God the Father,
And to the only begotten Son and to the Holy Ghost,
As it was in the beginning, is not and ever Shall be
world without end;
oh yes, Thank You, Lord, for Your love, kindness
And my new life in Christ!

How vivid I have Salvation endured –
Now I will gracefully Sing of His love, forevermore
In Jesus' precious name, Amen.

A New Verse to the Creator

God bestow that I may live
To compose for one more calm day,
And when the last word is created
I Thee ever so lovingly sing
When places within your mighty arms
As we rest gracefully encouraged
You'll smile alongside us all and rejoice
Naturally that we are tender enough to renew.

A Deep Calm

Calmed and Stilled
Allowing all beside peaceful waters
Letting every living thing praise Him above
Making me whole again.

THE LOVE OF JESUS

Return, let us retell God's beautiful love
It flows over like waves from out of the blue
We can't escape it, try as we shall
Yet it will pull at our feet, eternal to rest
His love is for everyone of us
To sing it, He died upon the Cross
His love will hold every joy we feel
We foretold the future, we foretold the facts
His love is like the brightest moon
To direct us far or near
Tell God that you trust Him now
Come into His arms O sinner, come home.

A Song of Devotion Unto God

My sacrifice, O God, is a broken spirit;
a broken and contrite heart you, God will not despise:

"Lord," I echoed, "I want to be Your servant, not yours truly.
So to everyone I bestow my pad, my gems – even my money."

Now, satisfied and pleased, I rested with a smile
And sung to God, "I bet it's been a perfect fourth
Since anyone has created a song – so naturally!"
His response amazed me, He rejoined, "not trembling."

Not an hour has passed by since the interval of time.
That somebody hasn't invented grace notes and chords,
Silver rods and staffs, masterpieces and pendants.
Tombstones and classics; still why not with righteousness!

"Just give me a teardrop- a soul ready to perform,
And I will offer them an intention, a song well-informed –
That a flame will be revived where there is simply breath
While their spirit will be restoreth by our comfort and
our time."

I waved my hands in the air and jumped across the shore.
It's tender to be open-voiced [I reflect my tastes are soft]
Yet it's worth the devotional to understand the beginning

That the cross isn't for anchors and Christ's love can't be beat.

2017

A Prayer of Unity

Behold, all Christians: "Endeavoring to keep the unity
Of the Spirit through the bond of peace."
Therefore, dear friends, from right now on:
When you hear us pray, our Jesus,
When you see us on our knees,
When you hear us calling, Jesus,
Hear us Jesus, if you please!
Absolutely without a second thought!
Every time we feel the unity of the Spirit
Moving within our hearts, we will pray!
We will pray! we will pray! we will pray!
Hereafter, friends, let's make every effort
To pray, if you will, Jesus, at all times;
And above all that, put on love,
Which is the perfect bond of unity.
How vividly I have Salvation related –
Now I will gracefully sing of His love, forevermore.
In Jesus' divine name, we pray, amen.

2018

Giving Rests

Promised Rest for God's People
All Who Enter into God's rest
will find rest from their labors, just
as God rested after creating the world.
                              Dink Simpson

Our Father Which Art in Heaven

Our Father which art in heaven
That's our song unto all nations
Our Father which art in heaven
Keep us safe
Safe to worship, work, play and love
We praise thee up above.

Lord, strengthen our trembling and weakness
Thoughts of imagination and our heartaches
Instruct us through You to be more graceful,
And voice Your tender peace even now.

May our raptures never pause with knowing Thee,
And may our guiding light be a symbol to others.

Thank You, God, for giving us our daily bread.
And lead us not into temptation.
Our Father which art in heaven, yes, we will pray,
Our Father which art in heaven
Let Your love remain in us completely.

2018

ALL TOLD

Christ the Savior is born
Hark the herald angels sing
Radiant beams from thy holy face
It came upon the midnight clear
Silent night, holy night
Thy glorious song above
Mary laid her child, lowly in a manger
All is calm, all is bright
Silent night, holy night
                    Earlisteen "Dink" Simpson

A Tender Melody unto God

Behold, Christians, "For you were bought at a price;
Therefore glorify God in your body and in your Spirit
which are God's."
And so, dear friends, as we rest upon all created things
Within Christ, So is He Himself.
Still ev'n when the trembling of life o'ertakes us
Hopes discouraged and fears disturbed
Ne'er Shall the cross forsake us;
Lo! it glows thro' peace and rapture,
Naturally this perfects the word of the Lord!
For He washed away our Sins, and withdrew the blues
He also made us whole;
After all god restores us, as He is the <u>Great Healer</u>
How thrilling I have Salvation rendered –
Now I will gracefully sing of His love, forevermore
In Jesus' divine name, we pray, amen.

Safely Home

Soon will the times of freedom be over;
Soon will everyone be carried along
By the current to eternity's shore.
Hold, now, loved ones, not a time
For taking a rest.
So, set up the life-boat and
Return us home today.
Set up the life-boat! Set up the life-boat
Some one is free, right here, right now.
Set up the life-boat! Set up the life-boat!
Some one had a taste for music.

The Poinsettia

Meditate the Poinsettia
For it's a symbol for chRistmas
The flower that stands for Love
But take deep thought!

Meditate the Poinsettia
And all that it stands for
The flower that flourishes Peace
For its felt in our hearts.

So, meditate the Poinsettia
May the flower thrive in Joy.
As we ponder over these things,
Then we may also ponderest the
well-known, Guiding Star.

Hail The Newborn King

Christ the savior is born

Heaven' star shone brightly forth

Radiant beams from Thy hold face

Infant holy, infant lowly

Sleep in heavenly peace

Tidings bringing, Hail the newborn King!

Mary laid here child in a manger; with the

Angels, let us sing Alleluia unto our King

Sleep in heavenly peace

An Easter Story

Easter is the wonderous story of old
Of God's great love toward men
When He first put in harmony
He great resurrection plan

For the Son of Thy love
Was Christ the purified lamb
Disgraced upon the cross of Calvary's hill
Yes, to redeem the full price of sinful men

Oh Easter is love in harmony
How grateful that love must be!
God gave His only begotten Son
Absolutely at peace and joy within His love

Easter is love in harmony
Whosoever believeth in Him
Shall have eternal life
Right now being washed from all my sin

Easter is love in harmony
No deeper love wilt be!
"For God so loved the world"
As He died to revive us and set us free.

Have a wonderful Easter

A TENDER SONG TO THE SAVIOR

Now I see in all creation
That the race is yet to the divine;
Naturally, I will say this: Seeing that
The race is alongside the tenderhearted.
Because the battling is not ours but God's
Still I see neither drink to the wise;
Neither riches to the foretelling,
Neither softness to the graceful,
Rather perfect love and singing,
Redirected throughout everyone of them.

A SONG OF PRAISE TO GOD

I s**E**e the Easter Lily blooming

Arising throughout the

Show, hear the angels

Swee**T**ly singing " Christ

Is aliv**E**" Alleluia! Have

A Wonde**R**ful Easter

BRAVERY AT ITS FINEST

On our nation's overcast day
The Statue of Liberty was a glow
Within joy's breadth we stood tall
To foretell bravery at its finest.
Now the nights have returned to days
Yet we will never forget the cost
Our love is clear
In everyone's faithful acts.
Naturally let us instead praise
The racing our hearts upheld
Life, Liberty, Happiness
As honor standing ablaze.
Still we see all of the blessings rendering
Beyond this great land for one, for all
That freedom and its sparkling symbols
Will always stand still.

HOME OF THE FREE

Let music swell the breeze,
And resound from sea to shining sea
Sweet home of the happy and free;
Let joyful voices burst into singing;
Let all that lives foretell;
Let lions their peace begin;
The roar echoing at all times –
Because of the brave.

A SONG OF PRAISE TO OUR SAVIOR

Into His hands we entrust our souls;
You have redeemed us, Lord, God of light.
Redirect us in spirit and truth
As You are the God who saves everyone.
Still we rest beside You the full day.
Your eyes are on the divine and
Your ears are open to our voices in care.
Naturally, we are not ashamed of the Gospel;
Because we believe, and we are certain
That nothing can ever change our conduct
For the softhearted.
Therefore, let's take up the Gospel and
Behold the return of His hands.
How sensational I have Salvation undergone –
Now I will joyfully sing to our Savior.

A Song of Thanksgiving

Thanksgiving ~~ *Thanks-living*
His divine will being softened as well;
As foretold we sail from light into light.
Now thank we all our God.
Know ye that the Lord is God
Sing songs with love and praise
Give thanks to the Lord of harvest
In tender fashion redirected, cause we're also
Voicing our love this Thanksgiving Day
Inside the flame my cup gracefully overflows
Now I will naturally sing of His love and
Give Him the glory, great things He hath done.

2017

Behold the Lamb

You, the Lamb
Oh soft one,
My heart doth sing
He shall our song unroll.
He has foreseen us through the night,
Through the day
And even as He looks over us
Or even when there is no light
He is our friend
Unto the very end
He is the one who created us
He knew that we
Were not faithful
How happy I have salvation undergone –
Now I will return singing with Him.

A Song of America

I might not at all served
        Nor worn the uniform
Still in my own uprightness
        I serve this sweet land also.

I love my country
I am this land's love.

Reflecting Upon the Cross

Reflecting upon **t**he cross

God forbid t**h**at I should boast

about anything **e**xcept the cross of

Our Lord Jesus **C**hrist. Because of

that cross, my inte**r**est in the world died

long ag**O**; and the world's

interest

in me i**s** also long dead.

May the grace of our **S**avior be with all of us.

A Class By Itself

Grace class is a class by itself

Rhythmics and scales are the Lord's; but

All the weights in the bag are His

Concern. Making the same for one another

Embrace with opened arms.

A Tender Chant unto the Savior

My surrender, O God, is a perfect spirit, a perfect
And full heart You, God will not overlook;
Therefore, dear friends, from this day forward
we should pray life this:
"And don't let us yield to temptation,
But deliver us from the evil one."
Sill yield not to temptation, as yielding is Sin;
Each victory will help us, Some other to win;
Fight manfully onward, dark passions tender;
Look e'er unto Jesus, He will carry e'eryone along
Absolutely, ask the Savior to help us,
Comfort us, strengthen and keep us;
He'll carry us along with Him, with Him
All the way;
Even so, let's pray and Seek Jesus' face
And turn from all my evil ways!

How sensational I have Salvation reencouraged –
Now I will gracefully sing of His love, forevermore.
In Jesus' divine name, we pray, Amen

"Lyric"

Behold, Lord, our every loves are known unto You:
In heaven's eternal rapture, the sweetest
Lyric is this: may Jesus be praised!
Let earth, sea and sky
From depth to height respond, may Jesus be praised
Ye universe of e'eryone, with out harmony held
May Jesus be praised! May Jesus be praised!
Absolutely, You, God, shall hear our voices in
The morning, in the morning we'll redirect it
Unto You, and we will chant a very tender song;
O Lord, in the morning, noon and at night!
Hereby we will chant and rejoice
And You, God, heard our voices!

How sensational I have Salvation reenraptured –
Now I will gracefully Sing of His love, forevermore
In Jesus' divine name, we pray, Amen.

This book is Dedicated in Loving Memory to My Mother,
Vera Celestia Loper Mobley

Me in 3rd Grade / 8 years old

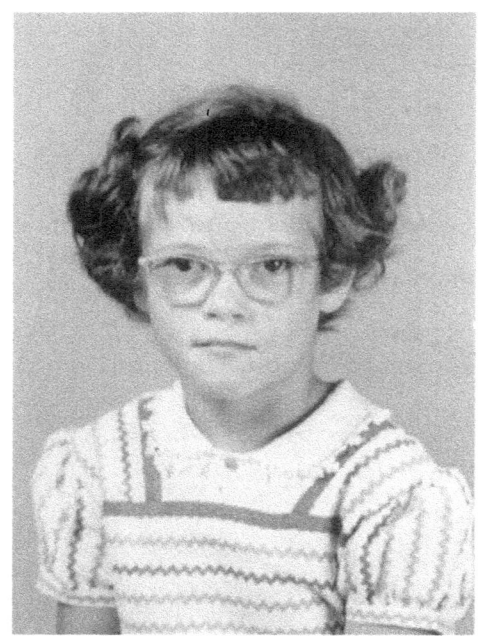

Graduate - Class of 1963 / 18 years old

Young Stephen - Our Only Child

My Husband Steve joined the US Army at age 19

My Wonderful Family
Steve and I have been Married Since September 14, 1973

www.ingramcontent.com/pod-product-compliance
Ingram Content Group UK Ltd.
Pitfield, Milton Keynes, MK11 3LW, UK
UKHW022237230426
12048UKWH00018BA/1314